The Robotx

Get Help from Simple Machines

Sloping
Up and Down

The Inclined Plane

Written by Felicia Law and Gerry Bailey   Illustrated by Mike Spoor

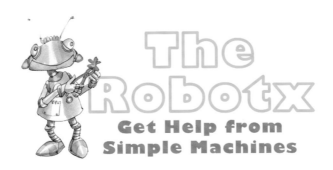

The Robotx

Get Help from Simple Machines

Crabtree Publishing Company
www.crabtreebooks.com
1-800-387-7650

PMB 59051, 350 Fifth Ave.
59ᵗʰ Floor,
New York, NY 10118

616 Welland Ave.
St. Catharines, ON
L2M 5V6

Published by Crabtree Publishing in 2014

Authors: Felicia Law and Gerry Bailey
Illustrator: Mike Spoor
Editor: Kathy Middleton
Proofreader: Crystal Sikkens
End matter: Kylie Korneluk
Production coordinator and
  Prepress technician: Ken Wright
Print coordinator: Margaret Amy Salter

Photographs:
All images are Shutterstock.com unless otherwise stated.
Pg 12 – holbox
Pg 18 – (t) max blain (b) Simon Krzic
Pg 19 – (t) Denizo71 (m) Brian Mitchell/Corbis
     (b) Jan Bruder
Pg 20/21 – Nickolay Vinokurov
Pg 27 – Local Favorite Photography

Printed in Canada/022014/MA20131220

Library and Archives Canada Cataloguing in Publication

Law, Felicia, author
    Sloping up and down : the inclined plane / written by Felicia Law and Gerry Bailey; illustrated by Mike Spoor.

(The robotx get help from simple machines)
Includes index.
Issued in print and electronic formats.
ISBN 978-0-7787-0419-5 (bound).--ISBN 978-0-7787-0425-6 (pbk.).--
ISBN 978-1-4271-7537-3 (pdf).--ISBN 978-1-4271-7531-1 (html)

    1. Inclined planes--Juvenile literature. I. Bailey, Gerry, author
II. Spoor, Mike, illustrator III. Title.

TJ147.L38 2014   j621.8   C2013-908715-X
                                        C2013-908716-8

Library of Congress Cataloging-in-Publication Data

CIP available at Library of Congress

Contents

The Robotx

Meet   and

RobbO   RobbEE

The robots' workshop

RobbO and RobbEE are usually very busy making useful machines in their workshop.

But today is different. The two robots plan to spend the day outside.

A machine is...

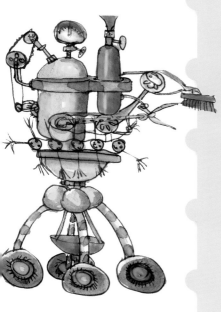

A machine is a tool used to make work easier. Work is the effort needed to create force. A force is a push or pull on an object. Machines allow us to push, pull, or lift a heavy weight much easier, or using less effort. All machines are made up of at least one **simple machine**.

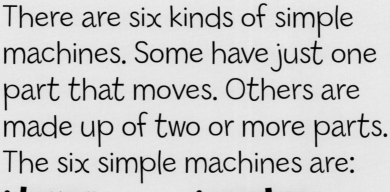

There are six kinds of simple machines. Some have just one part that moves. Others are made up of two or more parts. The six simple machines are:
- **lever**
- **wedge**
- **pulley**
- **screw**
- **inclined plane**
- **wheel and axle**

This book is about the inclined plane.

Today is a bit special. RobbO and RobbEE are off for a picnic in the hills.

RobbO is the guide. He has the easy job.

RobbEE is carrying the picnic basket. It's hard work, and very soon, he finds himself running out of power!

The hill is very steep.
RobbEE tries carrying.

He tries pulling.

He tries pushing.

But there is no easy way to
get everything up the hill.

Wait!
Maybe
there is!

Instead of taking the steep path STRAIGHT UP, RobbEE takes a gentle path off to the right.

Then he follows a gentle path off to the left, then to the right, then to the left...

RobbEE zigzags his way up
the hill on the gentle slopes.

The zigzag path is a lot longer than
the steep path. It takes more time
to walk, but RobbEE doesn't need
to use as much **effort**.

The easier path

A path that rises steeply from one point to another is difficult to climb.

Difficult!

A path that rises less steeply is easier to climb, but it does take longer!

Easy

A path that rises gently in a zigzag pattern is even easier, but it also takes even longer.

Very easy

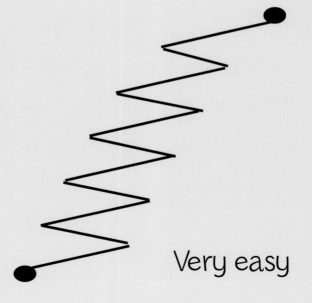

The story of Sisyphus

"At least we only had to climb the hill once," says RobbO. He tells his friend the story of Sisyphus.

Long, long ago, in ancient Greece, there was a king named Sisyphus. He was not a good king. He was dishonest, **sly**, and cruel.

In those days, the people believed in many gods. The gods could reward people who were good or punish them for being bad. King Sisyphus had behaved so badly he made the gods angry. They decided he must be punished.

When the king died, he went to live in the underworld where all humans went after death. But, as his punishment, he was forced by the gods to roll a heavy stone up a steep hill.

Every time he got to the top, the stone rolled back down to the bottom, and Sisyphus had to start again. He had to go on and on doing that forever.

Back in the workshop

After their picnic, it is time for the robots to tidy up inside.

RobbO is moving boxes. He climbs up and down the ladder.

It's a steep climb and the boxes are heavy.

RobbEE knows an easier way.
He changes the steep slope
into a gentler one using a ramp.

Now it's easy to push the
boxes up to the shelves.

Ramps

A sloping ramp like this is a simple machine known as an inclined plane. Inclined planes are flat surfaces that are tilted at an angle. One end of an inclined plane is higher than the other.

A ramp is a wedge shape.

This truck is being loaded using a ramp.

Lifting something very heavy can be difficult. A ramp makes it easier. It allows you to slide an object forward and upward a little at a time, until it reaches the right height.

Ramps help wheelchairs move up and down more easily than stairs.

A slide in a playground is an inclined plane.

Roads rise on gentle ramps to cross over one another.

Pyramid ramps

"Ramps have been around for thousands of years," says RobbO. "The ancient Egyptians used them to build the pyramids."

The pyramids at Giza in Egypt are **tombs** for kings. Thousands of people were needed to build them.

Higher and higher

RobbO explains how the pyramids were built.

Millions of tons of stone, such as granite and limestone, were cut from the ground in huge blocks. The blocks were pulled to the river by rolling them across logs.

The blocks were loaded onto boats which sailed up the Nile River to Giza. There, they were unloaded onto an inclined plane built right where the boats docked.

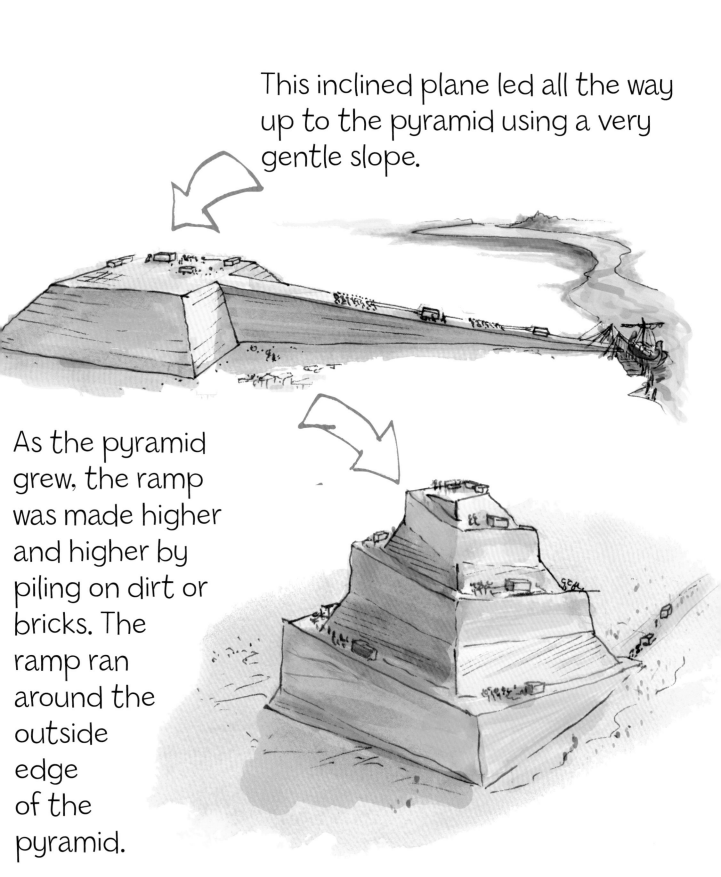

This inclined plane led all the way up to the pyramid using a very gentle slope.

As the pyramid grew, the ramp was made higher and higher by piling on dirt or bricks. The ramp ran around the outside edge of the pyramid.

Robb0's science workshop

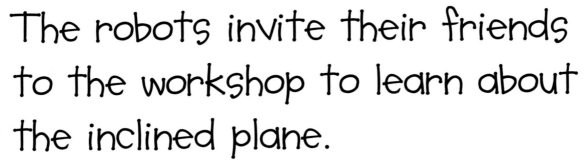

The robots invite their friends to the workshop to learn about the inclined plane.

load

When you lift something heavy, two forces are at work. One is the weight of the load pressing down. The other is you trying to lift it up. You are supplying the effort.

effort

effort

load

An inclined plane makes it easier to raise a weight because less effort is neede BUT the distance you must move the load is farther.

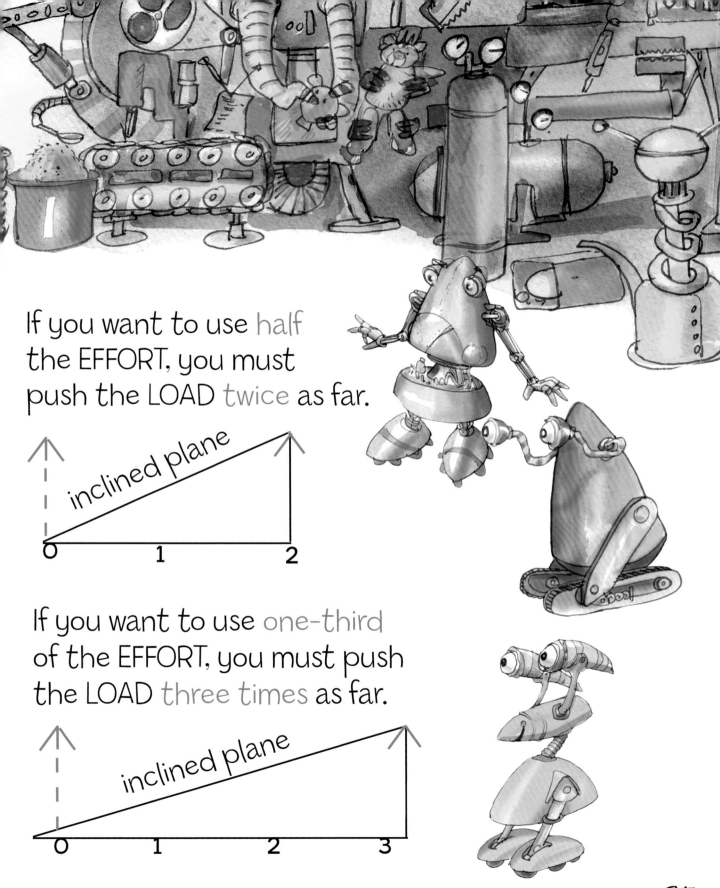

If you want to use half the EFFORT, you must push the LOAD twice as far.

inclined plane

0   1   2

If you want to use one-third of the EFFORT, you must push the LOAD three times as far.

inclined plane

0   1   2   3

Stairs and steps

Although a staircase is not a smooth slope like a ramp, it acts in the same way. A staircase works as an inclined plane, making it easier to climb. The longer and gentler the staircase, the easier it is to reach the top.

Ladders are inclined planes, too. Like stairs, they help people move from higher to lower places.

A ramp with steps helps the hen climb into the henhouse.

The longest staircase in the world is in Niesenbahn, Switzerland. It is 11,674 steps high and runs next to a railway that pulls cars up steep cliffs using cables.

The escalator

Sometimes two simple machines work together to make an even more useful machine. An escalator is a machine like this. It is made up of two simple machines: a wheel and axle, and an inclined plane.

handrail wheel

The stairs are upright when you stand on them, but flatten out to go around the wheels.

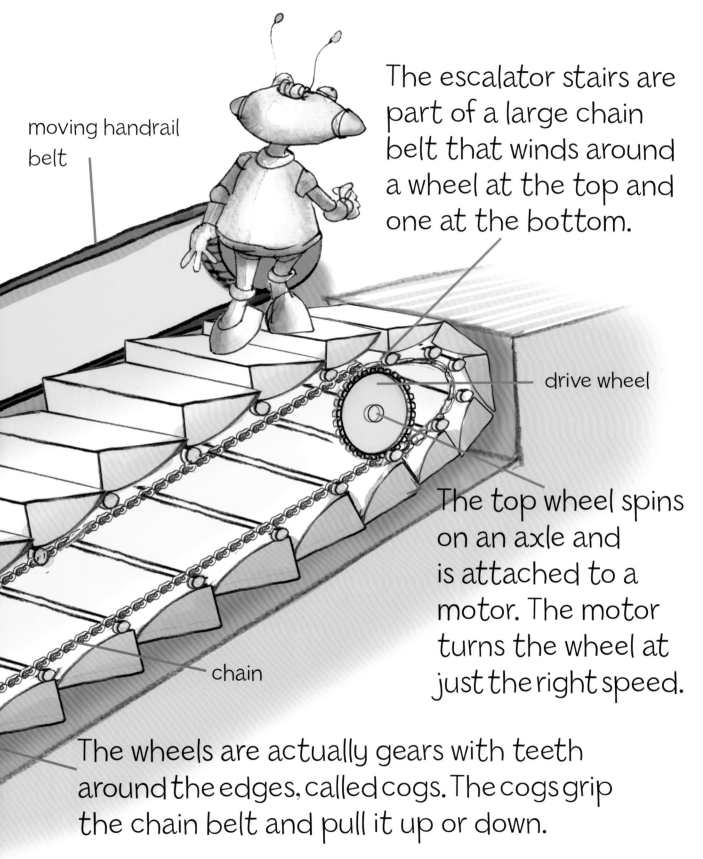

moving handrail belt

The escalator stairs are part of a large chain belt that winds around a wheel at the top and one at the bottom.

drive wheel

The top wheel spins on an axle and is attached to a motor. The motor turns the wheel at just the right speed.

chain

The wheels are actually gears with teeth around the edges, called cogs. The cogs grip the chain belt and pull it up or down.

29

The marble run

The Robotx have built a wonderful machine made up of lots and lots of ramps.

A marble run is an entertaining machine. It uses lots of ramps that work together. A marble is raised up to the top slope and is released so it will roll ramp by ramp to the bottom.

Learning more

Books

Inclined Planes
By Hope Collander
(Gareth Stevens Publishing, 2013)

Inclined Planes in Action
By Gillian Gosman
(PowerKids Press, 2010)

Get to Know: Inclined Planes
By Jennifer Christiansen
(Crabtree Publishing, 2009)

Put Inclined Planes to the Test
By Roseann Feldmann and Sally M. Walker
(Lerner Publishing Group, 2011)

Websites

www.mocomi.com/inclined-plane/
This website provides an animated physics video
and simple description of inclined planes.

teacher.scholastic.com/dirtrep/simple/plane.htm
A summary on inclined planes and how they work.

www.brainpop.com/technology/simplemachines
Brain Pop is an interactive website that provides
activities and information on inclined planes.

Glossary

inclined plane A slanted surface connecting a lower point to a higher point

lever A bar that rests on a support called a fulcrum which lifts or moves loads

pulley A simple machine that uses grooved wheels and a rope to raise, lower, or move a load

screw An inclined plane wrapped around a pole which holds things together or lifts materials

simple machine A machine that makes work easier by transferring force from one point to another

tombs A place where people are buried

wedge Two inclined planes joined together used to split things

wheel and axle A wheel with a rod, called an axle, through its center which lifts or moves loads

Index